GREEN DAY

Favorites to Strum and Sing

T0055446

ALBUM ARTWORK

American Idiot © 2004 Reprise Records for the U.S. and
WEA International Inc. for the world outside the U.S.

International Superhits © 2001 Reprise Records for the U.S. and
WEA International Inc. for the world outside the U.S.

Warning © 2000 Reprise Records for the U.S. and
WEA International Inc. for the world outside the U.S.

Nimrod © 1997 Reprise Records for the U.S. and
WEA International Inc. for the world outside the U.S.

Insomniac © 1995 Reprise Records for the U.S. and
WEA International Inc. for the world outside the U.S.

Dookie © 1994 Reprise Records for the U.S. and
WEA International Inc. for the world outside the U.S.

Kerplunk © 1991 Lookout Records

ISBN-10: 0-7390-4070-7
ISBN-13: 978-0-7390-4070-6

CONTENTS

4

AMERICAN IDIOT

Words by BILLIE JOE
Music by GREEN DAY

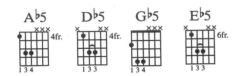

Intro:

(Riff A)- - - - - - - - - - - - - - - - - - ⌐ (Riff B) - - - - - - - - - - - - - - - - - - - ⌐

4/4 ‖: A♭5 D♭5   G♭5 | D♭5 A♭5 G♭5 | A♭5   D♭5   G♭5 | D♭5 A♭5   :‖

Verse 1:

N.C.   A♭5 (w/Riff A)

Don't want   to   be   an   American idiot.

N.C.   A♭5 (w/Riff B)

Don't want   a   nation under the   new   media.

N.C.   A♭5 (w/Riff A)

Hey,   can   you   hear   the   sound   of   hysteria?

N.C.   A♭5 (w/Riff B)

The   subliminal mind - f**k   America.

Chorus:

D♭5   A♭5

Welcome   to   a   new   kind   of   tension   all   across   the   alienation,

E♭5   A♭5

Where   everything   isn't   meant   to   be   o - kay.

D♭5   A♭5

Television dreams of tomorrow,   we're not the ones who're meant to follow,

E♭5 | N.C. | | A♭5 (w/Riffs A & B) | ‖

For   that's   enough   to   argue.

Verse 2:

N.C.   A♭5 (w/Riff A)

Well,   maybe   I'm   the   f**got   America.

N.C.   A♭5 (w/Riff B)

I'm   not   part   of   a   redneck agenda.

N.C.   A♭5 (w/Riff A)

Now,   everybody,   do   the   propaganda,

N.C.   A♭5 (w/Riff B)

And   sing   along   to   the   age   of   paranoia.

Chorus:

  D♭5   A♭5
    Welcome to a new kind of tension   all across the alienation,

  E♭5   A♭5
    Where everything isn't meant to be o - kay.

  D♭5   A♭5
    Television dreams of tomorrow,   we're not the ones who're meant to follow,

  E♭5 | N.C. | | A♭5 *(w/Riffs A & B) 2 times* ‖
    For that's enough to argue.

Guitar Solo:

                                            1.   2.

‖: D♭5 | | A♭5 | | E♭5 | | A♭5 | :‖ A♭5 *(w/Riff B) 2 times* ‖

Verse 3:

  A♭5   D♭5   G♭5   D♭5 A♭5
    Don't want to be an Ameri-can idiot,

  A♭5   D♭5   G♭5   D♭5   A♭5
    One nation con - trolled by the media.

  A♭5   D♭5   G♭5 D♭5   A♭5 N.C.
    Infor-mation age of hys - teria   is calling out to idiot America.

Chorus:

  D♭5   A♭5
    Welcome to a new kind of tension   all across the alienation,

  E♭5   A♭5
    Where everything isn't meant to be o - kay.

  D♭5   A♭5
    Television dreams of tomorrow,   we're not the ones who're meant to follow,

  E♭5   A♭5 *(w/Riff B)*
    For that's enough to argue.

Outro:

                                   1.   2.

‖: A♭5 D♭5 G♭5 | D♭5 A♭5 G♭5 | A♭5 D♭5 G♭5 | D♭5 A♭5 :‖ A♭5 D♭5 G♭5 | D♭5 A♭5 ‖

BASKET CASE

Lyrics by BILLIE JOE
Music by GREEN DAY

Tune down 1/2 step:
⑥ = E♭ ③ = G♭
⑤ = A♭ ② = B♭
④ = D♭ ① = E♭

E B C#m G# A D

Verse 1:

$\frac{4}{4}$

E				B		C#m		G#	
Do	you	have	the	time	to	listen	to	me	whine

A				E			B	
A - bout	nothing	and	everything	all	at	once.		

E				B		C#m		G#	
I	am	one	of	those	mel - odramatic		fools;		

A				E			B	
Neu - rotic,	to	the	bone,	no	doubt	about	it.	

Chorus:

A			B		E	
Sometimes	I	give	myself	the	creeps.	

A			B			E
Sometimes	my	mind	plays	tricks	on	me.

A		B		E		D		C#m
It	all	keeps	adding	up,	I	think	I'm	cracking up.

A		B	
Am	I	just	para - noid? Am I just stoned?

E	B		C#m	B		E	B		C#m	B

Verse 2:

E			B		C#m		G#	
I	went	to	a	shrink	to	analyze	my	dreams.

A				E			B	
She	says	it's	lack	of	sex	that's	bringing me	down.

E			B		C#m		G#	
I	went	to	a	whore,	he	said	my	life's a bore.

A			E			B	
So	quit	my	whining	'cause	it's	bringing her	down.

Chorus:

A   B   E
Sometimes I give myself the creeps.

A   B   E
Sometimes my mind plays tricks on me.

    A   B   E   D   C♯m
It all keeps adding up, I think I'm cracking up.

    A   B
Am I just para - noid? Yeah, yeah, yeah.

‖: E B | C♯m B | E B | C♯m B :‖

Bridge:

A   B   N.C.
Grasping to con - trol so I better hold...

Instrumental:

‖: E B | C♯m G♯ | A E | B | :‖
on.

Chorus:

A   B   E
Sometimes I give myself the creeps.

A   B   E
Sometimes my mind plays tricks on me.

    A   B   E   D   C♯m
It all keeps adding up, I think I'm cracking up.

    A   B
Am I just para - noid? Am I just stoned?

Outro: *Play 4 times*

‖: E | C♯m | A E B :‖ A E B ‖

BRAIN STEW

Lyrics by BILLIE JOE
Music by GREEN DAY

Tune down 1/2 step:
⑥ = E♭ ③ = G♭
⑤ = A♭ ② = B♭
④ = D♭ ① = E♭

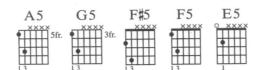

Intro:

$\frac{4}{4}$ ‖: A5　　　　G5　　│　F♯5　　　　　　F5　　　E5　　　:‖

Verse 1:

A5　　　　　　G5　　　　　　　F♯5　　F5　　E5
I'm　having　trouble　trying　to　　sleep.

A5　　　　　　G5　　　　　　　　F♯5　　F5　　E5
I'm　counting　sheep　but　running　out.

A5　　　　　　　G5　　　F♯5　　　　　　　F5　　E5
As　time　ticks　by,　　　　　　and　still　I　　try.

A5　　　　　　G5　　　　　　　F♯5　　F5　　　　　E5
No　rest　for　crosstops　in　my　mind.　On　my　own. Here　we　go.

‖: A5　　　　G5　　│　F♯5　　　　　　F5　　　E5　　　:‖

Verse 2:

A5　　　　　　　G5　　　　　　　　F♯5　　F5　　E5
My　eyes　feel　like　they're　gonna　　bleed,

A5　　　　　　　G5　　　　　F♯5　　F5　　E5
Dried　up　and　bulging　out　my　　skull.

A5　　　　　　G5　　　F♯5　　　　　　　F5　　E5
My　mouth　is　dry,　　　　my　face　is　numb.

A5　　　　　　G5　　　　　　　F♯5　　F5　　　　E5
F***ed　up　and　spun　out　in　my　room.　On　my　own. Here　we　go.

‖: A5　　　　G5　　│　F♯5　　　　　　F5　　　E5　　　:‖

Verse 3:

A5		G5		F#5	F5	E5

My mind is set on over - drive.

A5		G5		F#5	F5	E5

The clock is laughing in my face.

A5		G5	F#5		F5	E5

A crooked spine, my sense is dulled.

A5		G5	F#5	F5		E5

Passed the point of deliri - um. On my own. Here we go.

‖: A5   G5 | F#5   F5   E5 :‖

Verse 4:

A5		G5		F#5	F5	E5

My eyes feel like they're gonna bleed,

A5		G5		F#5	F5	E5

Dried up and bulging out my skull.

A5		G5	F#5		F5	E5

My mouth is dry, my face is numb.

A5		G5		F#5	F5	E5

F***ed up and spun out in my room. On my own. Here we go.

Outro:

Play 6 times

hold throughout

Brain Stew - 2 - 2
25508

BOULEVARD OF BROKEN DREAMS

Words by BILLIE JOE
Music by GREEN DAY

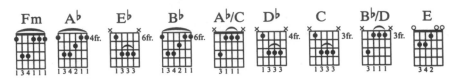

Intro:

4/4 ‖: Fm   A♭ | E♭   B♭   :‖

Verse 1:

Fm   A♭   E♭   B♭
I   walk   a   lonely   road,   the   only   one   that   I   have   ever   known.

Fm   A♭   E♭   B♭
Don't know where it goes, but it's home to me   and I walk alone.

| Fm   A♭ | E♭   B♭ |

Fm   A♭   E♭   B♭
I   walk   this   empty   street   on   the   boulevard   of   broken   dreams,

Fm   A♭   E♭   B♭
Where the city sleeps and I'm the only one   and I walk alone.

Fm A♭ E♭   B♭
I   walk   alone,   I   walk   alone.

Fm A♭ E♭   B♭   A♭/C
I   walk   alone,   I   walk   a...

Chorus:

D♭   A♭   E♭   Fm
My   shadow's   the   only   one   that   walks   beside   me.

D♭   A♭   E♭   Fm
My   shallow   heart's   the   only   thing   that's   beating.

Db   Ab   Eb   Fm
Sometimes   I wish   someone out there   will find me.

Db   Ab   C
'Til then   I walk   alone.

‖: Fm   Ab | Eb   Bb   :‖

Verse 2:

Fm   Ab   Eb   Bb
I'm walking down the line that divides me somewhere in my mind.

Fm   Ab   Eb   Bb
On the borderline of the edge and whereI walk alone.

| Fm   Ab | Eb   Bb |

Fm   Ab   Eb   Bb
Read be- tween the lines of what's f***ed up and everything's alright.

Fm   Ab   Eb   Bb
Check my vital signs and know I'm still alive and I walk alone.

Fm Ab Eb   Bb
I walk alone,   I walk alone.

Fm Ab Eb   Bb   Ab/C
I walk alone,   I walk a...

Chorus:

Db   Ab   Eb   Fm
My shadow's the only one that walks beside me.

Db   Ab   Eb   Fm
My shallow heart's the only thing that's beating.

Db   Ab   Eb   Fm
Sometimes I wish someone out there will find me.

Db   Ab   C
'Til then I walk   alone.

|: Fm   A♭ | **1.** E♭   B♭ :|| **2.** E♭   B♭ ||

I walk alone,   I walk a...

Guitar Solo:

|: D♭   A♭ | **1.2.3.** E♭   Fm :|| **4.** C | ||

Verse 3:

Fm   A♭   E♭   B♭

I walk this empty street on the boulevard   of broken dreams,

Fm   A♭   E♭   B♭   A♭/C

Where the city sleeps and I'm the only one   and I walk a...

Chorus:

D♭   A♭   E♭   Fm

My shadow's the only one that walks   beside me.

D♭   A♭   E♭   Fm

My shallow heart's   the only thing   that's beating.

D♭   A♭   E♭   Fm

Sometimes I wish   someone out there   will find me.

D♭   A♭   C | ||

'Til then I walk   alone.

Outro:

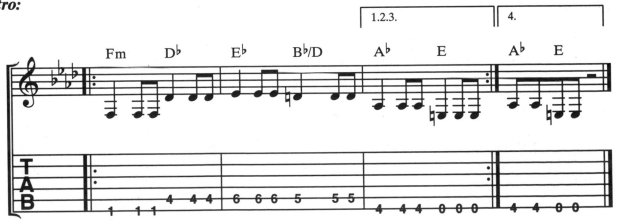

HOLIDAY

Words by BILLIE JOE
Music by GREEN DAY

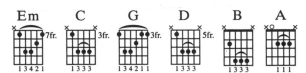

Intro:

Play 3 times

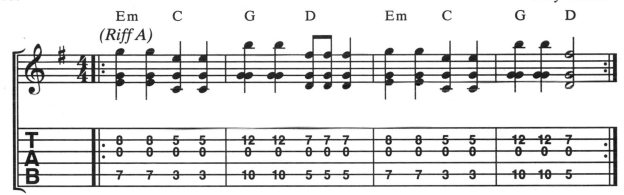

*To match recording, place capo at the 1st fret.

Verse 1:

Em			C		G	D	
Hear	the	sound	of	the	falling	rain	

Em		C		G	B	Em
Coming	down	like	an	Arma - geddon	flame.	

	C	G		D		B
The	shame, the	ones	who	died	with - out	a	name.

Em		C	G	D	
Hear	the	dogs	howling	out	of	key

Em		C	G		B
To	a	hymn	called	"Faith and	misery,"

Em	C	G	D		B
And	bleed,	the	company	lost	the	war	today.

Chorus:

Em		C		G		D
I	beg	to	dream and	differ	from the	hollow lies.

Em		C		G		B
This	is	the	dawn - ing	of	the	rest of our lives	on holiday.

(w/Riff A)

Em	C		G	D		Em	C		G	D	‖

14

Verse 2:

Em		C		G	D	
Hear	the	drum	pounding	out	of	time,

Em		C	G		B	Em
Another	protest- or	has	crossed	the	line

C		G	D		B	
To	find	the	money's	on	the	other side.

Em		C		G	D	
Can	I	get	an - other	"A - men?"		

Em		C		G	B	Em
There's	a	flag	wrapped a - round	a	score	of men.

C		G	D		B	
A	gag,	a	plastic bag	on	a	monument.

Chorus:

Em		C		G		D
I	beg	to	dream and	differ	from the	hollow lies.

Em			C	G		B
This	is	the	dawn - ing	of	the	rest of our lives on holiday.

Interlude:

Em   G   C A D B   Em   G   D B Em
(Riff B)

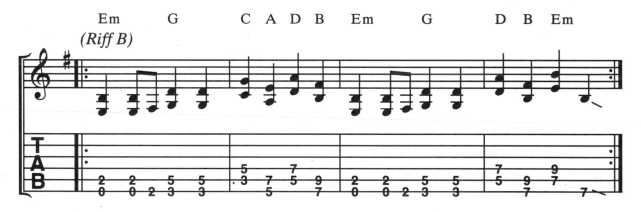

Guitar Solo:

| C | G | B | Em D | C | G | B | | | | ‖ |

(w/Riff B)
| Em | | | | |

(w/Riff B)
Em

The   representative from   California   has   the   floor.

Holiday - 3 - 2
25508

Bridge:

Em *(w/Riff B, 4 times)*

Zeig Heil to the President gasman, bombs away is your punishment.

Pulverize the Eiffel Towers, who criticize your government.

Bang, bang goes the broken glass and kill all the fags that don't agree.

Trials by fire setting fire is not a way that's meant for me.

B

Just 'cause,   just 'cause, because we're outlaws, yeah.

Chorus:

Em		C		G		D

I beg to dream and differ from the hollow lies.

Em			C		G		B

This is the dawn - ing of the rest of our lives.

Em		C		G		D

I beg to dream and differ from the hollow lies.

Em			C		G		B

This is the dawn - ing of the rest of our lives...

This is our lives on holiday.

Outro:

(w/Riff A)

‖: Em   C | G   D | Em   C | G   D :‖ 1. | 2. D   B   Em ‖

Holiday - 3 - 3
25508

GOOD RIDDANCE (TIME OF YOUR LIFE)

Lyrics by BILLIE JOE
Music by BILLIE JOE and GREEN DAY

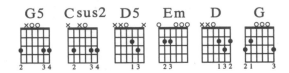

Intro:

Verse 1:

G5   Csus2   D5
Another turning point, a   fork   stuck   in   the   road.

G5   Csus2   D5
Time grabs you by the wrist, di - rects you where to go.

Em   D   Csus2   G
So make the best of this test and don't ask why.

Em   D   Csus2   G
It's not a question, but a lesson learned in time.

Chorus:

Em   G5   Em   G5
It's something unpre - dictable but in the end is right.

Em   D
I   hope you had the time of your life.

‖: G5 ———— | | Csus2 | D5 :‖

Verse 2:

G5   Csus2   D5
So take the photographs and still frames in your mind.

G5   Csus2   D5
Hang it on a shelf in good health and good time.

Em   D   Csus2   G
Tattoos of memories, and dead skin on trial.

Em   D   Csus2   G
For what it's worth, it was worth all the while.

Chorus:

Em   G5   Em   G5
It's something unpre - dictable but in the end is right.

Em   D
I hope you had the time of your life.

‖: G5 | | Csus2 | D5 :‖

Interlude:

| G5 | | Csus2 | D5 | G5 | | Csus2 | D5 |

| Em D | | Csus2 G | | Em D | | Csus2 G | ‖

Chorus:

Em   G5   Em   G5
It's something unpre - dictable but in the end is right.

Em   D
I hope you had the time of your life.

‖: G5 | | Csus2 | D5 :‖

Chorus:

Em   G5   Em   G5
It's something unpre - dictable but in the end is right.

Em   D
I hope you had the time of your life.

1.   2.
             rit.
‖: G5 | | Csus2 | D5 :‖ D5 | G5 | ‖

Good Riddance (Time of Your Life) - 2 - 2
25508

HITCHIN' A RIDE

Lyrics by BILLIE JOE
Music by GREEN DAY

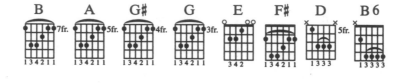

Intro:

$\frac{4}{4}$ ‖: B   A | G♯   G   :‖

Verse 1:

B   A   G♯   G   B   A   G♯   G
Hey, mister, where you headed?   Are you in a hurry?

B   A   G♯   G   B   A   G♯   G
I need a lift to happy hour, say, oh no.

B   A   G♯   G   B   A   G♯   G
Do you break for distilled spirits? I need a break as well.

B   A   G♯   G   B   A   G♯   G
The well that in - ebri - ates the guilt. One, two. One, two, three, four.

Play 3 times

‖: B   A | G♯   G   :‖ B   A | G♯   N.C.   ‖

Verse 2:

B   A   G♯   G   B   A   G♯   G
Cold turkey's getting stale, tonight I'm eating crow.

B   A   G♯   G   B   A   G♯   G
Fer - mented salmo - nella, poison oak, no.

B   A   G♯   G   B   A   G♯   G
There's a drought at the fountain of youth, and now I'm dehy - drated.

B   A   G♯   G   B   A   G♯   G
My tongue is swelling up, I say, one, two. One, two, three, four.

Play 4 times

‖: B   A | G♯   G   :‖

Chorus:

```
    E           F#          B           A       G#        G
        Troubled  times,   you   know   I    cannot   lie.

    E                                           F#
        I'm    off    the    wagon   and   I'm   hitchin'  a    ride.
```

‖: B   A | G#   G   :‖

Verse 3:

```
    B           A           G#          G      B           A     G#     G
        There's  a   drought  at   the  fountain  of  youth,    and  now  I'm  dehy- drated.

    B     A       G#      G                  | N.C.                   |                      ‖
        My   tongue  is   swelling  up,   I   say...
```

Guitar Solo: *Play 8 times*

‖: B   D | G   F#   :‖

Chorus:

```
    E           F#          B           A       G#        G
        Troubled  times,   you   know   I    cannot   lie.

    E                                           F#
        I'm    off    the    wagon   and   I'm   hitchin'  a    ride.
```

Outro: *Play 7 times*

```
‖: B                 D          | G                    F#              :‖
   (ride.)                                  Hitch  -  in'        a
```

```
 | B             A          | G#          N.C.       | B 6                        ‖
   (ride.)
```

JADED

Lyrics by BILLIE JOE
Music by GREEN DAY

Tune down 1/2 step:
⑥ = E♭ ③ = G♭
⑤ = A♭ ② = B♭
④ = D♭ ① = E♭

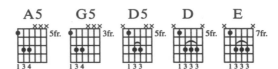

A5   G5   D5   D   E

Intro: *Play 4 times*

¢ ‖: A5 | G5   D5   :‖

Verse 1:

A5   G5   D5   A5   G5   D5
Somebody keep my balance, I think I'm falling off

A5   G5   D5   A5 G5   D5
Into a state of regres - sion.

A5   G5   D5   A5   G5   D5
The expi - ration date rap - idly coming up.

A5   G5   D5   A5
It's leaving me be - hind to rank.

Chorus:

D

Always move forward.

                                                    A5   G5   A5   G5   A5
Going "straight" will get you nowhere.

D

There is no progress.

                              E
Evolution killed it all.   I found my place in nowhere.

‖: A5 | G5   D5   :‖

Verse 2:

A5   G5   D5   A5   G5   D5
I'm taking one step sideways, leading with my crutch.

A5   G5   D5   A5   G5   D5
Got a f***ed up equi - libri - um.

```
A5                        G5      D5      A5              G5   D5
    Count down from  nine  to    five.  Hoo - ray!  We're gonna  die.

A5              G5   D5    A5
    Blessed  in - to    extinc - tion.
```

Chorus:

```
    D
        Always  move   forward.

                                    A5      G5  A5    G5  A5
        Going  "straight" will   get    you   nowhere.

    D
        There  is     no    progress.

                            E
        Evolution  killed   it    all.     I    found  my   place  in   nowhere.
```

Interlude: *Play 7 times*

```
‖: A5              | G5      D5     :‖ A5              |              ‖
```

Chorus:

```
    D
        Always  move   forward.

                                    A5      G5  A5    G5  A5
        Going  "straight" will   get    you   nowhere.

    D
        There  is     no    progress.

                            E
        Evolution  killed   it    all.     I    found  my   place  in   nowhere.
```

Outro:

```
A5          G5   D5          A5          G5   D5
                    You're  nowhere.

        A5      G5   D5   A5        G5   D5   A5
You're  no            -          where.
```

LONGVIEW

Lyrics by BILLIE JOE
Music by GREEN DAY

E   D   B   A

Tune down 1/2 step:
⑥ = E♭ ③ = G♭
⑤ = A♭ ② = B♭
④ = D♭ ① = E♭

Intro:

4/4 : Bass guitar
(E) | (D) | (E) | (D)   :|

Verse 1:

Bass guitar
(E)   (D)   (E)   (D)
I sit a - round and watch the tube but nothing's on.

(E)   (D)   (E)   (D)
I change the channels for an hour or two,

(E)   (D)   (E)
Twiddle my thumbs just for a bit.

         (D)   (E)
I'm sick of all the same old s***;

       Guitar enters
    (D)   (E)   D
In a house with unlocked doors, and I'm f***ing lazy.

Chorus:

B   A   E   B
Bite my lip and close my eyes.

       A   E
Take me a - way to paradise.

B   A   E   B
I'm so damn bored, I'm going blind

         A
And I smell like s***.

Bass guitar
| (E) | (D) | (E) | (D) ‖

Verse 2:

Bass guitar

(E)				(D)			(E)			(D)	
	Peel	me	off	this	velcro	seat	and	get	me	moving.	

(E)				(D)			(E)		(D)	
	I	sure	as	hell	can't	do	it	by	myself.	

(E)				(D)			(E)	
	I'm	feeling	like	a	dog	in	heat,	

		(D)				(E)	
Barred	in -	doors	from	the	summer	street.	

Guitar enters

							(D)				(E)			D	
I	locked	the	door	to	my	own	cell	and	I	lost	the	key.			

Chorus:

B			A		E		B
	Bite	my	lip	and	close	my	eyes.

			A		E	
Take	me	a -	way	to	paradise.	

B			A		E	B
	I'm	so	damn	bored, I'm	going	blind

				A	
And	I	smell	like	s***.	

Bridge:

E			D	
I	got	no	motivation.	

E			D	
Where	is	my	motivation?	

E				D	
No	time	for	a	motivation.	

E			D	
Smoking	my	inspiration.		

Interlude:

Play 3 times

‖: B | A E :‖ B | A ‖

Bass guitar

(E) | (D) | (E) | (D) ‖

Verse 3:

Bass guitar

(E)			(D)			(E)			(D)	
	I	sit	a - round	and	watch	the	phone	but	no	one's	calling.

(E)			(D)			(E)			(D)	
	Call	me	pa - thetic,	call	me	what	you	will.		

(E)			(D)			(E)	
	My	mother	says	to	get	a	job,

(D)		(E)
But	she	don't	like	the	one	she's	got.

(D)	(E)	D	A
When	mastur - bation's	lost	its	fun,	you're	f***ing	lonely.

Chorus:

B   A   E   B
Bite   my   lip   and   close   my   eyes.

            A   E
Take   me   a -   way   to   paradise.

B   A   E   B
I'm   so   damn   bored,   I'm   going   blind

       A   E
And   loneli - ness   has   to   suffice.

B   A   E   B
Bite   my   lip   and   close   my   eyes.

        A   E
Oh,   slippin' a -   way   to   paradise.

B   A   E   B
Some   say   quit   or   I'll   go   blind

        A
But   it's   just   a   myth.

Outro:

Repeat and fade

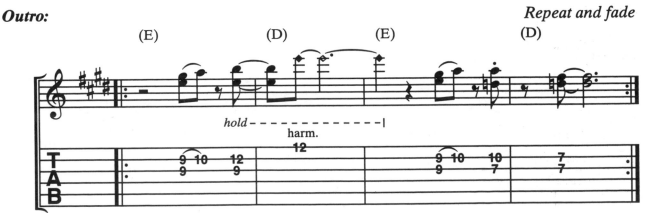

MINORITY

Lyrics by BILLIE JOE
Music by GREEN DAY

Intro:

(Riff)

Chorus:

C   F   G   F
I want to be the mi - nori - ty.
C   F   G   F
I don't need your au - thori - ty.
C   F   G   F
Down with the moral ma - jori - ty.
     C   F   G   F
'Cause I want to be the mi - nori - ty.

Verse 1:

     C   G   F   C
I pledge al - legience to the under - world.
           G   F   G
One nation under - dog there of which I stand a - lone.
     C   G   F   C
A face in the crowd, un - sung against the mold.
           F   G   C
Without a doubt, singled out, the only way I know.

Chorus:

     C   F   G   F
'Cause I want to be the mi - nori - ty.
C   F   G   F
I don't need your au - thori - ty.
C   F   G   F
Down with the moral ma - jori - ty.
     C   F   G   F
'Cause I want to be the mi - nori - ty.

26

Bridge:

```
    Am              E     F     C
    Stepped out     of    the   line

    Am              E     F        G
    Like a     sheep runs from the   herd.

    Am              E     F     C
    Marching out    of    time

    Am              F     G                                    B
    To   my   own  beat  now.    The   only  way  I    know.
```

Verse 2:

```
            C       G     F           C
    One  light, one  mind flashing in  the   dark.
                    G               F          G
    Blinded by  the  silence of  a   thousand broken hearts.
            C       G     F               C
    "For  crying out  loud,"     she  screamed unto  me.
                        F         G                   C
    A   free - for - all,  f*** 'em  all.  "You  are  your  own  sight."
```

Chorus:

```
            C               F           G   F
    'Cause I    want  to   be   the   mi - nori - ty.
    C       F           G   F
    I    don't need your au - thori - ty.
    C               F       G   F
    Down with  the   moral ma - jori - ty.

            C               F           G   F
    'Cause I    want  to   be   the   mi - nori - ty.
```

Instrumental:

```
| Am   E | F  C | Am   E | F  G | Am   E | F  C | Am   F | G    |    B ‖
```

Interlude:

```
| C    G    | F    C    |    G    | F    G    ‖
```

Minority - 3 - 2
25508

Verse 3:

```
        C              G    F              C
One  light,  one   mind  flashing  in    the    dark.
                     G              F            G
Blinded  by    the   silence  of   a    thousand broken  hearts.
           C         G      F              C
"For   crying  out   loud,"    she   screamed unto   me.
                     F              G              C
A    free - for - all,  f*** 'em  all.  "You  are  your  own  sight."
```

Chorus:

```
        C              F            G    F
'Cause  I    want  to    be    the   mi - nori - ty.
C           F            G    F
I    don't need  your  au - thori - ty.
C              F          G    F
Down with   the    moral ma - jori - ty.
        C              F            G    F
'Cause  I    want  to    be    the   mi - nori - ty.
C              F            G    F
I    want  to    be    the   mi - nori - ty.
C              F            G    F
I    want  to    be    the   mi - nori - ty.
C              F            G    F
I    want  to    be    the   mi - nori - ty.
C              F            G    F
I    want  to    be    the   mi - nori - ty.
```

Outro:

```
(w/Riff)                                              rit.
| C       G     | F     C     |        G     | F     C     ‖
```

MACY'S DAY PARADE

Words by BILLIE JOE
Music by GREEN DAY

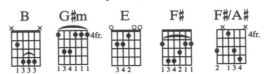

B   G#m   E   F#   F#/A#

Intro:

4/4 | B | | ||

Verse 1:

B

Today's the   Macy's Day   Parade.

G#m

The   night   of   the   living   dead   is   on   its   way.

E   F#   B

With   a   credit   report   for   the   duty   call.

It's   a   lifetime   guarantee,

G#m

Stuffed   in   a   coffin,   "ten   percent   more   free."

E   F#   B

Red   light   special   at   the   mauso- leum.

Pre-chorus:

E

Give   me   something   that   I   need.

F#   E

Satisfaction   guaranteed   to   you.

What's   the   consolation   prize?

F#   B

Economy - sized   dreams   of   hope.

Verse 2:

B

When   I   was   a   kid,   I   thought

G#m

I   wanted   all   the   things   that   I   haven't   got.

E   F#   B

Oh,   but   I   learned   the   hardest   way.

G#m

Then   I   realized   what   it   took

```
                                                        E
To   tell   the   difference between thieves  and   crooks.
        F#                B
Let's learn, me    and   you.
```

Pre-chorus:

```
    E
        Give   me   something that   I     need.
F#
        Satisfaction guaranteed.
```

Chorus:

```
                    B                F#/A#      G#m
'Cause I'm  thinking 'bout  a    brand - new  hope,
        F#              E
The   one   I've  never  known.
                    F#                    B
'Cause now   I    know  it's   all   that  I    wanted.
```

Instrumental:

```
‖: B        |           | G#m       |           | E     | F#      | B       |           :‖
```

Pre-chorus:

```
    E
        What's  the   consolation prize?
F#                                  E
        Economy - sized  dreams  of   hope.

Give   me   something that   I     need.
F#
        Satisfaction  guaranteed.
```

Chorus:

```
                    B                F#/A#      G#m
'Cause I'm  thinking 'bout  a    brand - new  hope,
        F#              E                   F#
The   one   I've  never  known and   where it    goes.
                    B                F#/A#  G#m
And    I'm  thinking 'bout  the   only    road,
        F#              E                      F#
The   one   I've  never  known and   where it    goes.
                    B                F#/A#      G#m
And    I'm  thinking 'bout  a    brand - new  hope,
        F#              E
The   one   I've  never  known.
                    F#                    B
'Cause now   I    know  it's   all   that  I    wanted.
```

Macy's Day Parade - 2 - 2
25508

NICE GUYS FINISH LAST

Lyrics by BILLIE JOE
Music by BILLIE JOE and GREEN DAY

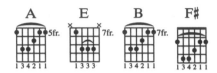

Intro:

Verse 1:

```
        E
Nice  guys  finish  last.  You're  running  out  of  gas.
             B                              E         A
Your  sympathy  will  get  you  left  be - hind.
             E
Some - times  you're  at  your  best  when  you  feel  the  worst.
             B                                              E
You  feel  washed  up,  like  piss  goin'  down  the  drain.
```

Pre-chorus:

```
    A                                     E
Pressure  cooker,  pick  my  brain  and  tell  me  I'm  insane.
    A                                     E
I'm  so  f***ing  happy,  I  could  cry.
    A                                     E
Every  joke  can  have  its  truth,  but  now  the  joke's  on  you.
        F#                              B
I  never  knew  you're  such  a  funny  guy.
```

Chorus:

```
        E          A      E              A
Oh,  nice  guys  finish  last,  when  you  are  the  out - cast.
        E              A                      B      A
Don't  pat  yourself  on  the  back,  you  might  break  your  spine.
```

Verse 2:

E

Living on command. You're shaking lots of hands.
      B   E   A

You're kissing up and bleeding all your trust.

E

Taking what you need. Bite the hand that feeds.
      B   E

You'll lose your memory and you got no shame.

Pre-chorus:

A   E

Pressure cooker, pick my brain and tell me I'm insane.

A   E

I'm so f***ing happy, I could cry.

A   E

Every joke can have its truth, but now the joke's on you.
   F#   B

I never knew you're such a funny guy.

Chorus:

     E   A   E   A

Oh, nice guys finish last, when you are the out - cast.
      E   A   B

Don't pat yourself on the back, you might break your spine.
     E   A   E   A

Oh, nice guys finish last, when you are the out - cast.
      E   A   B   A

Don't pat yourself on the back, you might break your spine.

Interlude:

| E | A | B | | A | E | | A | B | | A | E | | A | B |
| | A | E | | A | | | F# | | B | | | |

Chorus:

     E   A   E   A

Oh, nice guys finish last, when you are the out - cast.
      E   A   B

Don't pat yourself on the back, you might break your spine.
     E   A   E   A

Oh, nice guys finish last, when you are the out - cast.
      E   A   B   A

Don't pat yourself on the back, you might break your spine.

| E | | | A | E |

STUCK WITH ME

Lyrics by BILLIE JOE
Music by GREEN DAY

Tune down 1/2 step:

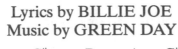

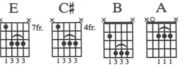

Intro:

```
4
4 : E        |        C#  B    A  |          |          : 
```

Verse 1:

```
E                          B
I'm  not  part  of   your  elite, I'm  just  alright.

A           B              A                  B
Class  structures, waving  colors,  bleeding  from  my  throat.

E                          B
Not  subservient  to  you,  I'm  just  alright.

A               B                A                  B
Down  classed  by  the  powers  that  be,  give  me  loss  of  hope.
```

Chorus:

```
C#m              A      E
Cast  out,  buried  in  a  hole.

C#m              A       E
Struck  down,  forcing  me  to  fall.

C#m              A        E
Destroyed,  giving  up  the  fight.

           A      B      E
Well,  I  know  I'm  not  al - right.
```

Verse 2:

```
E                                        B
What's  my  price  and  will  you  pay  it  if  it's  alright?

A                B              A                  B
Take  it  from  my  dignity  and  waste  it  'til  it's  dead.

E                                B
Throw  me  back  into  the  gutter  'cause  it's  alright.

A           B              A                  B
Find  another pleasure f***er,  drag  'em  down  to  hell.
```

Chorus:

C#m   A   E
Cast out, buried in   a   hole.

C#m   A   E
Struck down, forcing me   to   fall.

C#m   A   E
Destroyed, giving up   the   fight.

          A   B   E
Well, I   know I'm not al - right.

Instrumental:

```
           1.2.3.    4.
‖: E  |    C# B A |   |  :‖  One,  two,  three,  four! |

| B   |          |         |          |          ‖
```

Chorus:

C#m   A   E
Cast out, buried in   a   hole.

C#m   A   E
Struck down, forcing me   to   fall.

C#m   A   E
Destroyed, giving up   the   fight.

          A   B   E
Well, I   know I'm not al - right.

REDUNDANT

Lyrics by BILLIE JOE
Music by BILLIE JOE and GREEN DAY

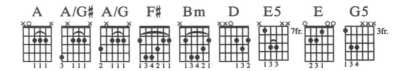

Intro: *(Riff)*

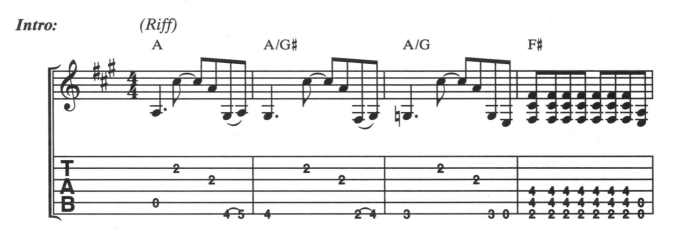

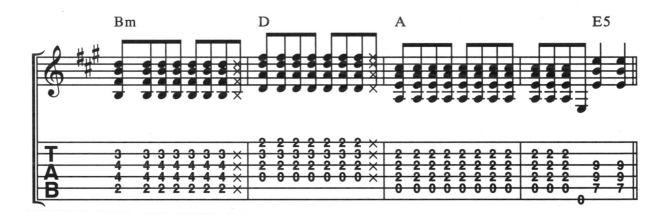

Verse 1:

A   D   A   D   A

We're living in   repe - tition.

                D   E   G5

Content in   the   same   old   shtick a - gain.

A   D   A   D   A

Now   routine's turning to   con - tention.

                D   E

Like a   produc-tion line going over and   over and   over, roller coaster.

Chorus: *(w/Riff)*

```
            A                 A/G♯
Now   I   cannot speak.  I've  lost   my   voice.

A/G                  F♯
 Speechless  and   re - dundant.


            Bm                  D
'Cause  I   love  you's  not  e - nough.

              A         E5
I'm   lost  for   words.
```

Verse 2:

```
A          D                   A        D   A
   Choreo - graphed  and   lack   of   passion.

       D              E        G5
Proto - types  of   what  we   were.

A          D              A       D   A
   One  full   circle  till   I'm   nauseous.

          D                E
Taken  for   granted  now.  I've  waste  it,  faked  it,  ate  it.  Now  I   hate  it.
```

Chorus: *(w/Riff)*

```
            A                 A/G♯
'Cause  I   cannot speak.  I've  lost   my   voice.

A/G                  F♯
 Speechless  and   re - dundant.

          Bm                   D
'Cause  I   love  you's  not  e - nough.

              A         E5
I'm   lost  for   words.
```

Instrumental:

| A | D | A D | A | F♯ | Bm | E | G5 |

| A | D | A | | F♯ | Bm E | | ‖ |

Chorus: *(w/Riff, simile)*

      A   A/G♯

Now   I   cannot speak. I've   lost   my   voice.

A/G   F♯

Speechless and   re - dundant.

      Bm   D

'Cause I   love   you's   not   e - nough.

        A

I'm   lost   for   words.

      (w/Riff, simile)

      A   A/G♯

Now   I   cannot speak. I've   lost   my   voice.

A/G   F♯

Speechless and   re - dundant.

      Bm   D

'Cause I   love   you's   not   e - nough.

        A

I'm   lost   for   words.

Outro:

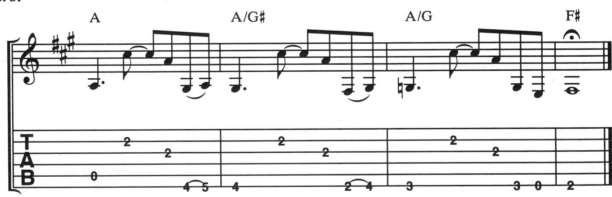

WALKING CONTRADICTION

Lyrics by BILLIE JOE
Music by GREEN DAY

A5   D   G5

Tune down 1/2 step:
⑥ = E♭ ③ = G♭
⑤ = A♭ ② = B♭
④ = D♭ ① = E♭

Intro:

4/4 | A5 | | | | ‖

Verse 1:

```
A5        D         G5           A5
Do   as   I    say,  not   as   I    do
                     D         G5       A5
Because  the  s***'s  so   deep  you  can't  run   away.
            D     G5      A5
I    beg   to  differ,  on   the  contrary,
            D      G5          A5
I    agree  with  every  word  that  you   say.
            D         G5        A5
Talk  is   cheap  and  lies  are   expensive,
              D         G5          A5
My    wallet's  fat  and  so   is   my   head.
            D         G5          A5
Hit   and  run,  and  then  I'll  hit   you   again,
              D       G5          A5
A    smart  a**  but   I'm   playing  dumb.
```

| A5   D   G5 | A5 | | D   G5 | A5 | ‖

Verse 2:

```
A5    D         G5    A5
Standards  set   and   broken  all   the   time,
          D     G5       A5
Control  the  chaos  behind  the  gun.
          D     G5       A5
Call   it   as   I   see   it,   even  if
          D     G5         A5
I    was  born  deaf,  blind  and  dumb.
```

```
        D       G5              A5
Losers  winning big     on    the   lottery,

        D       G5          A5
Rehab  rejects  still   sniffing  glue.

        D       G5    A5
Constant refu - tation  with    myself,

          D            G5           A5
A    victim  of    a    catch  twenty  two.
```

Chorus:

```
D   G5  A5
              I    have   no    belief,

D   G5  A5                              D      G5   A5
              But  I   believe  I'm   a   walking  contra - diction.

        D            G5          A5
And  I   ain't  got   no    right.
```

```
| A5        D        G5 |      A5        |          D      G5 |      A5        ||
```

Verse 3:

```
A5        D        G5              A5
Do   as   I    say,  not   as   I   do
                          D            G5          A5
Because  the   s***'s  so   deep   you   can't   run   away.

           D     G5          A5
I    beg   to    differ,  on   the    contrary,
                 D     G5              A5
I    agree  with  every  word  that   you   say.

           D           G5        A5
Talk  is   cheap  and   lies   are   expensive,

           D            G5            A5
My    wallet's  fat   and   so    is   my   head.

           D           G5            A5
Hit  and  run,  and   then  I'll   hit   you   again,

                 D     G5           A5
A    smart  a**  but   I'm   playing  dumb.
```

Chorus:

```
D   G5  A5
              I     have  no    belief,
D   G5  A5                          D    G5    A5
              But  I    believe  I'm   a    walking  contra - diction.
         D          G5         A5
And  I     ain't  got   no    right.
D   G5  A5
              I     have  no    belief,
D   G5  A5                          D    G5    A5
              But  I    believe  I'm   a    walking  contra - diction.
         D          G5         A5
And  I     ain't  got   no    right.
```

Outro:

```
| A5        D       G5 |    A5        |      D     G5 |    A5        |

|           D    G5 |    A5        |      D     G5 |    A5         ‖
```

WAITING

Words and Music by BILLIE JOE, ANTHONY HATCH and GREEN DAY

Tune down 1/2 step:
⑥ = E♭ ③ = G♭
⑤ = A♭ ② = B♭
④ = D♭ ① = E♭

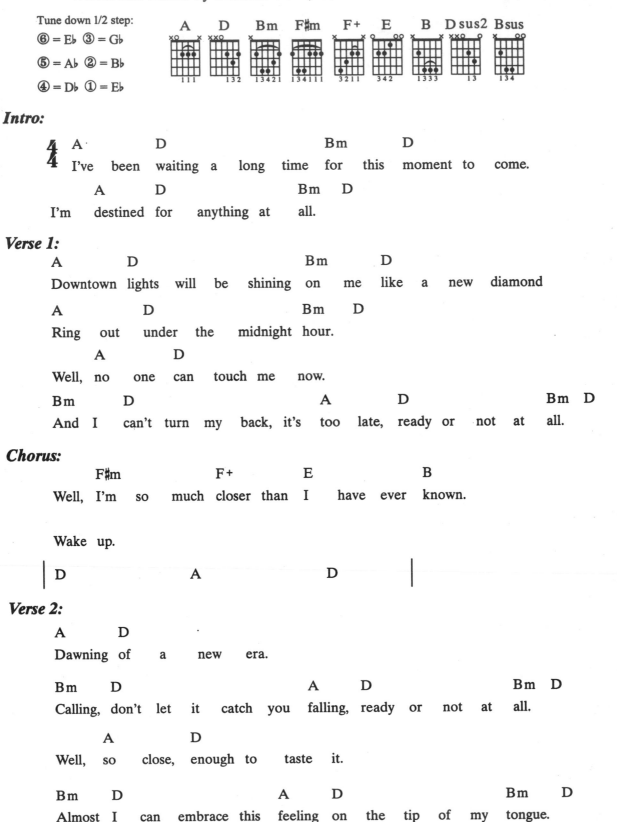

Intro:

$\frac{4}{4}$
```
A                D                    Bm        D
I've been waiting a  long  time  for  this  moment to  come.
       A      D              Bm    D
I'm destined for  anything at   all.
```

Verse 1:
```
A           D                Bm          D
Downtown lights will be shining on  me  like  a   new  diamond
A           D                Bm    D
Ring   out   under the  midnight hour.
        A        D
Well, no  one  can  touch me  now.
Bm       D                    A      D              Bm  D
And  I  can't turn  my  back, it's  too  late, ready or  not  at  all.
```

Chorus:
```
     F#m              F+         E              B
Well, I'm  so  much closer than  I  have  ever  known.


Wake   up.

| D           A        D          |                           ‖
```

Verse 2:
```
A      D
Dawning of   a   new  era.

Bm    D                       A      D          Bm  D
Calling, don't let  it  catch you  falling, ready or  not  at  all.
       A        D
Well,  so   close, enough to   taste  it.

Bm    D                       A      D          Bm        D
Almost I  can  embrace this  feeling on  the  tip  of  my  tongue.
```

Chorus:

F#m   F+   E   B
Well, I'm so much closer than I have ever known.

Wake up.

D A D	A D A D A	D A D	A D A D A
			Bet - ter thank your

D A D	A D A D A	D A D E
Luck - y stars.	Sure, hey, hey.	

Guitar Solo:

A	D	Bm	D	A	D	Bm	D

Chorus:

F#m   F+   E   B
Well, I'm so much closer than I have ever known.

Wake up.

D A D	A D A D A	D A D	A D A D A
			Bet - ter thank your

D A D	A D A D A	D A D E
Luck - y stars.	Sure, hey, hey.	

Interlude:

A	Dsus2	Bsus	Dsus2

Midtro:

A   Dsus2   Bsus Dsus2
I've been waiting a lifetime for this moment to come.

   A   Dsus2   Bsus Dsus2
I'm destined for anything at all.

Verse 3:

A   D
Dumbstruck, color my stupid.

Bm   D   A   D   Bm   D
Good luck, you're gonna need it where I'm going if I get there at all.

     A   D Bm   D
Wake up.

        A   D   Bm   D
Better thank your lucky stars.

WAKE ME UP WHEN SEPTEMBER ENDS

Words by BILLIE JOE
Music by GREEN DAY

Verse 1:

G5   G5/F♯   G5/E   G5/D
Summer has come and passed, the innocent can never last.

C   Cm   G5
Wake me up when September ends.

               G5/F♯   G5/E   G5/D
Like my father's come to pass, seven years has gone so fast.

C   Cm   G5   G5/F♯
Wake me up when September ends.

Chorus:

Em   Bm   C   G5   G5/F♯
Here comes the rain again, falling from the stars.

Em   Bm   C   D
Drenched in my pain again, be - coming who we are.

Verse 2:

G5   G5/F♯   G5/E   G5/D
As my memo - ry rests, but never forgets what I lost.

C   Cm   G5
Wake me up when September ends.

Interlude:

(w/Riff)   *Play 3 times*
‖: G5   :‖

Verse 3:

```
G5              G5/F#                      G5/E          G5/D
Summer  has   come   and   passed,   the   innocent  can   never  last.

C               Cm                       G5
Wake   me   up   when   September  ends.

                     G5/F#         G5/E                    G5/D
Ring   out   the   bells   again,   like   we   did   when   spring   began.

C               Cm                       G5    D/F#
Wake   me   up   when   September  ends.
```

Chorus:

```
Em              Bm             C                        G5       D/F#
Here   comes   the   rain   again,   falling   from   the   stars.

Em              Bm                   C                        D
Drenched   in   my   pain   again,   be - coming   who   we   are.
```

Verse 4:

```
G5              G5/F#                      G5/E          G5/D
As   my   memo - ry     rests,   but   never   forgets   what   I     lost.

C               Cm                       G5    D/F#
Wake   me   up   when   September  ends.
```

Guitar Solo:

Em	Bm	C	G5 D/F#	Em	

| Bm | C | Dsus | D | Dsus | D | |

Interlude:

(w/Riff)

‖: G5 | :‖

Verse 5:

```
G5              G5/F#                      G5/E          G5/D
Summer  has   come   and   passed,   the   innocent  can   never  last.

C               Cm                       G5
Wake   me   up   when   September  ends.

                     G5/F#                 G5/E            G5/D
Like   my   father's   come   to   pass,   twenty   years   has   gone   so   fast.

C               Cm                       G5
Wake   me   up   when   September  ends.

C               Cm                       G5
Wake   me   up   when   September  ends.

C               Cm                       G5
Wake   me   up   when   September  ends.
```

WARNING

Words by BILLIE JOE
Music by GREEN DAY

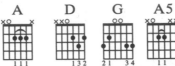

Intro:　　　　　　(Riff A)　　　　　　　　　　　　　　　*Play 4 times*

A　　　　　　　　　D　　　　　　　G　　　　　　　D

Verse 1:　　　　　　(w/Riff A, 8 times)

A　　　　　D
This is a public ser - vice announcement.

G　　　　　D　　　　　A D G D
This is on - ly a test.

　　　A　　D　　　G　　　D　　　A D G D
E - mergen - cy, e - vacuation, protest.

　　　　　A　　　D　　　G　　　　D
May im - pair your ability to operate ma - chinery.

A　　　D　　　G　　　　　D
Can't quite tell just what it means to me.

A　　　　D　　　　　G　　　　　　　D
Keep out of reach of children, don't you talk to strangers.

　　　　A　　D　　　G　　　　　D
Get your philoso - phy from a bumper sticker.

Chorus:

(w/Riff A, 4 times)

A　D　G　　　D　　　A　D　G D
Warn - ing: Live without warning.

　　　　　A　　D　G　　　　D
Let's see a warn - ing: Live without warning.

A　　D　G　　　D
Without. Alright.

Interlude: *(Riff B)*

(w/Riff A)

||: A   D | G   D   :||

Verse 2:

(w/Riff A, 8 times)

A   D   G   D   A   D   G   D
Better   homes   and   safety - sealed   com - munities.

A   D   G   D   A   D   G   D
Did   you   re - member to   pay   the   u - tilities?

A   D   G   D
Caution: Police   line.   You   better   not   cross.

                         A   D   G   D
Is   the   cop   or   am   I   the   one   that's really dangerous?

A   D   G   D
Sanitation, expiration date,   question everything?

A.   D   G   D
Or   shut   up   and   be   a   victim of   au - thority.

Chorus:

(w/Riff A, 8 times)

A   D   G   D   A   D   G   D
Warn - ing: Live   without   warning.

                         A   D   G   D   A   D   G   D
Let's   see   a   warn - ing: Live   without   warning.

                         A   D   G   D   A   D   G   D
Let's   see   a   warn - ing: Live   without   warning.

                         A   D   G   D
Let's   see   a   warn - ing: Live   without   warning.

A   D   G   D
                         Without.   Alright.

46

Interlude:

    (w/Riff B)

‖: A5 | :‖

Verse 3:

(w/Riff B, 4 times)
A5
Better homes and safety- sealed communities.

Did you remember to pay the utilities?

(w/Riff A, 4 times)
A   D   G   D
Caution: Police line. You better not cross.
              A   D   G   D
Is the cop or am I the one that's really dangerous?
A   D   G   D
Sanitation, expiration date, question everything?

A   D   G   D
Or shut up and be the victim of au - thority.

Chorus:

(w/Riff A, 8 times)
A   D   G   D   A   D   G   D
Warn - ing: Live without warning.
             A   D   G   D   A   D   G   D
Let's see a warn - ing: Live without warning.
             A   D   G   D   A   D   G   D
Let's see a warn - ing: Live without warning.

             A   D   G   D   A   D   G   D
Let's see a warn - ing: Live without warning.

Outro: *(w/Riff A)*
                  A   D
This is a public ser - vice announcement.

G   D   A
This is on - ly a test.

WELCOME TO PARADISE

Lyrics by BILLIE JOE
Music by GREEN DAY

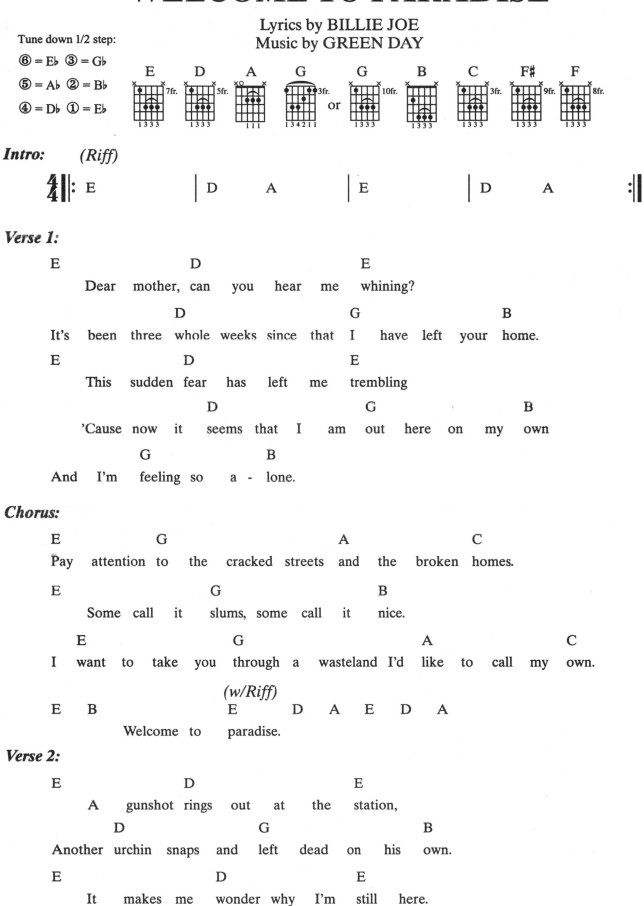

Tune down 1/2 step:

⑥ = Eb ③ = Gb

⑤ = Ab ② = Bb

④ = Db ① = Eb

Intro: *(Riff)*

$\frac{4}{4}$ ‖: E | D A | E | D A :‖

Verse 1:

```
        E                    D              E
    Dear  mother, can   you   hear   me   whining?
                         D              G              B
It's  been  three  whole  weeks  since  that  I   have  left  your  home.
    E                    D              E
    This  sudden  fear  has   left   me   trembling
                         D              G              B
    'Cause  now  it   seems  that  I   am   out   here   on   my   own
                 G             B
And  I'm  feeling  so    a - lone.
```

Chorus:

```
    E          G               A          C
Pay  attention to  the  cracked  streets  and   the   broken  homes.
    E                 G              B
    Some  call   it   slums,  some  call   it   nice.
        E                 G              A          C
I  want  to  take  you  through  a   wasteland  I'd  like  to  call  my  own.
                         (w/Riff)
    E   B               E       D   A   E   D   A
        Welcome  to   paradise.
```

Verse 2:

```
    E                    D              E
    A  gunshot  rings  out   at    the    station,
        D              G              B
Another  urchin  snaps  and  left  dead  on   his   own.
    E                    D              E
    It  makes  me   wonder  why  I'm  still  here.
```

                       D   G   B
For some strange reason it's now feeling like my home

                     G   B
And I'm never gonna go.

Chorus:

E   G   A   C
Pay attention to the cracked streets and the broken homes.

E   G   B
   Some call it   slums, some call it   nice.

   E   G   A   C
I want to take you through a wasteland I'd like to call my own.

                              (w/Riff, 2 times)
E B   E   D A E D A E D A E D A
   Welcome to   paradise.

Interlude:

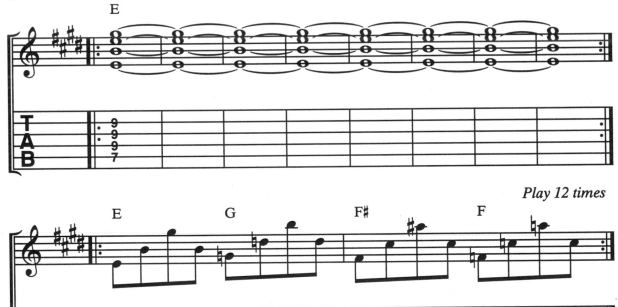

Play 12 times

Verse 3:

  E   D   E
   Dear mother, can you hear me laughing?

              D   G   B
It's been six whole months since that I have left your home.

  E   D   E
   It makes me wonder why I'm still here.

```
                          D                G                B
For   some   strange   reason   it's   now   feeling   like   my   home

                          G           B
And   I'm   never   gonna   go.
```

Chorus:

```
    E                G                     A                C
Pay   attention   to   the   cracked   streets   and   the   broken   homes.

    E                        G                        B
        Some   call   it   slums,   some   call   it   nice.

        E                        G                     A                        C
I   want   to   take   you   through   a   wasteland   I'd   like   to   call   my   own.
```

(w/Riff, 2 times)
```
E   B                        E       D   A   E   D   A
        Welcome   to   paradise.

        E       D   A   E   D   A   E
Oh,   paradise.
```

WHEN I COME AROUND

Lyrics by BILLIE JOE
Music by GREEN DAY

Tune down 1/2 step:

⑥ = E♭   ③ = G♭

⑤ = A♭   ② = B♭

④ = D♭   ① = E♭

G   D   Em   C   A5   C5

Intro: *(Riff)* *Play 3 times*

Verse 1:

(w/Riff, 8 times)

G   D   Em C G   D   Em C
   I   heard you crying loud   all   the   way across town.

        G   D   Em   C
You've been searching for that someone, and it's me, out on the prowl.

        G   D   Em   C
As you sit a - round feeling sor - ry   for your - self,

G   D   Em C G   D   Em C
   Well, don't get lonely now,   and dry your whining eyes.

        G   D   Em   C
I'm just roaming for the moment sleazing my backyard so don't get

        G   D   Em   C
So uptight, you been thinking about ditching me.

Chorus:

A5   C5
   No   time   to   search the   world   around

A5   C5
   'Cause you know where I'll be found when I   come around.

(w/Riff, 2 times)

| G   D | Em   C | G   D | Em   C |

© 1994 WB MUSIC CORP. (ASCAP) and GREEN DAZE MUSIC (ASCAP)

Verse 2:

(w/Riff, 8 times)

```
  G          D                Em   C  G         D                  Em    C
    I  heard  it  all  be - fore,       so  don't  knock  down  my  door.
```

```
          G              D            Em              C
I'm  a    loser  and  a   user  so  I   don't  need  no   ac - cuser
```

```
     G              D            Em           C
To   try  and  slag  me  down  because  I  know  you're  right.
```

```
  G          D                Em  C  G       D                Em    C
    So  go  do  what  you  like.       Make  sure  you  do  it  wise.
```

```
          G                D            Em              C
You  may  find  out  that  your  self - doubt  means  nothing  was  ever  there.
```

```
       G              D            Em          C
You  can't  go  forcing  something  if  it's  just  not  right.
```

Chorus:

```
  A5                          C5
    No  time  to  search  the   world  around
```

```
  A5                              C5
    'Cause  you  know  where  I'll  be  found  when  I  come  around.
```

(w/Riff, 2 times)

```
| G        D      | Em    C      | G      D      | Em      C              ||
                                                          Ooh!
```

Guitar Solo:

(w/Riff, 2 times)

```
| G        D      | Em    C      | G      D      | Em      C              ||
```

Chorus:

```
  A5                          C5
    No  time  to  search  the   world  around
```

```
  A5                              C5
    'Cause  you  know  where  I'll  be  found  when  I  come  around.
```

(w/Riff, 4 times)

```
G    D    Em    C
           Oh,  when  I    come  around.
```

```
G    D    Em    C
           Oh,  when  I    come  around.
```

```
G    D    Em    C                        G    D    Em    C
           When  I    come  around.
```

GEEK STINK BREATH

Lyrics by BILLIE JOE
Music by GREEN DAY

Tune down 1/2 step:
⑥ = E♭ ③ = G♭
⑤ = A♭ ② = B♭
④ = D♭ ① = E♭

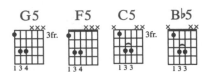

G5   F5   C5   B♭5

Intro: *Play 4 times*   *Play 4 times*

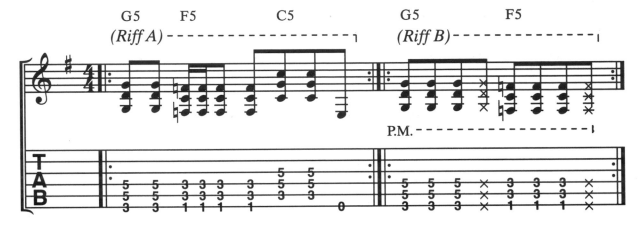

Verse 1:

      G5   F5   G5   F5
I'm on a mission. I made my de - cision,

      G5   F5   G5   F5
Lead a path of self destruc - tion.

      G5   F5   G5   F5
A slow pro - gression, killing my com - plexion

       G5 F5   G5
And it's rotting out my teeth.

Pre-chorus:

B♭5   F5   B♭5   F5
I'm on a roll, no self - con - trol,

B♭5   F5   B♭5   F5
I'm blowing off steam with meth - ampheta-mine.

Chorus:

       G5   F5   G5   F5
Well, don't know what I want 'cause that's all that I've got.

```
          G5            F5         G5
And   I'm   picking  scabs   off   my   face.
```

(w/Riff B)
```
| G5                    F5           | G5                F5           ‖
```

Verse 2:

```
  G5        F5        G5              F5
Every      hour  my   blood  is   turning  sour

            G5                F5        G5     F5
And   my   pulse  is   beating  out   of   time.

      G5      F5              G5            F5
I   found  a   treasure  and   it's   filled  with   sick   pleasure

        G5            F5        G5
And   it   sits   on   a   thin,  white  line.
```

Pre-chorus:

```
B♭5              F5        B♭5            F5
I'm  on  a   roll,        no   self - con - trol,

      B♭5          F5                B♭5   F5
I'm   blowing  off   steam   with   meth - ampheta-mine.
```

Chorus:

```
          G5            F5            G5            F5
Well,  don't  know  what  I    want  'cause  that's  all    that   I've   got.

          G5          F5        G5
And   I'm   picking  scabs   off   my   face.
```

Interlude: *Play 7 times*

(w/Riff A)
```
‖: G5     F5        C5      :‖ G5     F5        C5            ‖
                                                      I'm
```

Geek Stink Breath - 3 - 2
25508

Verse 3:

```
G5            F5           G5              F5
On    a    mission. I    got    no    de - cision,
```

```
         G5              F5           G5          F5
Like   a     cripple  running  the    rat    race.
```

```
G5           F5           G5              F5
Wish  in   one  hand  and   s***   in    the    other,
```

```
         G5              F5           G5
And   see   which  one   gets   filled   first.
```

Pre-chorus:

```
Bb5            F5          Bb5            F5
I'm   on   a    roll,     no    self - con - trol,
```

```
    Bb5          F5                  Bb5     F5
I'm   blowing  off    steam   with    meth - ampheta-mine.
```

Chorus:

```
          G5              F5              G5             F5
Well,  don't  know  what  I    want  'cause  that's  all   that  I've   got.
```

```
          G5           F5          G5
And   I'm   picking  scabs  off   my    face.
```

Outro:

```
     (w/Riff A)
‖: G5 F5  C5  | G5 F5  C5  :‖ G5   F5   C5  | G5   F5   C5  | G5         ‖
                              Geek              stink          breath.
```

J.A.R. (JASON ANDREW RELVA)

Words by BILLIE JOE
Music by GREEN DAY

Tune down 1/2 step:
⑥ = E♭   ③ = G♭
⑤ = A♭   ② = B♭
④ = D♭   ① = E♭

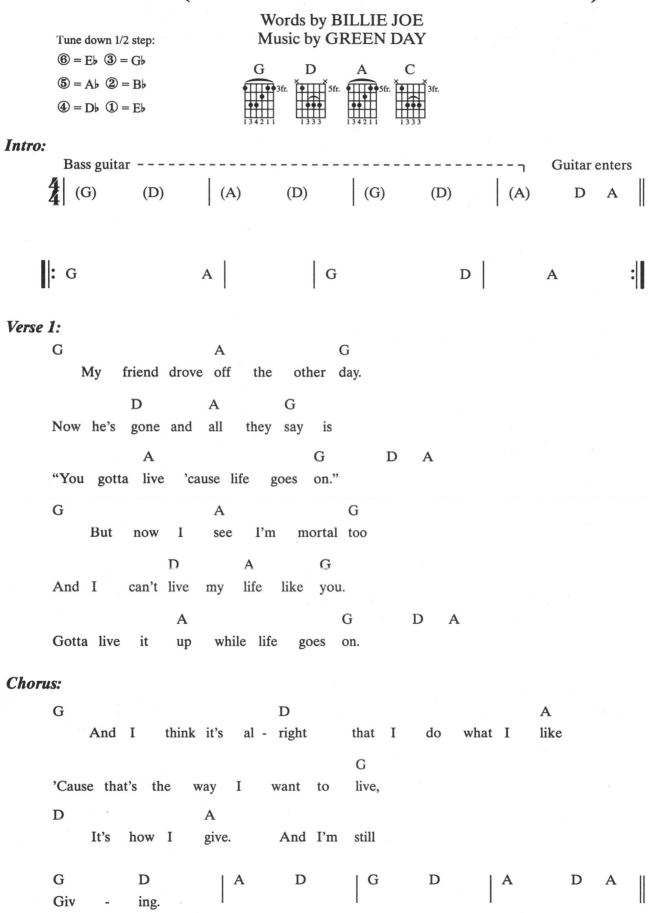

Intro:

Bass guitar - Guitar enters

4/4 (G)   (D)   │ (A)   (D)   │ (G)   (D)   │ (A)   D   A   ‖

‖: G   A   │   │ G   D │   A   :‖

Verse 1:

G   A   G
 My   friend   drove   off   the   other   day.

     D   A   G
Now   he's   gone   and   all   they   say   is

    A   G   D   A
"You   gotta   live   'cause   life   goes   on."

G   A   G
 But   now   I   see   I'm   mortal   too

    D   A   G
And   I   can't   live   my   life   like   you.

    A   G   D   A
Gotta   live   it   up   while   life   goes   on.

Chorus:

G   D   A
 And   I   think   it's   al - right   that   I   do   what   I   like

            G
'Cause   that's   the   way   I   want   to   live,

D   A
 It's   how   I   give.   And   I'm   still

G   D   │ A   D   │ G   D   │ A   D   A   ‖
Giv - ing.

Verse 2:

```
      G                    A                    G
        And   now   I   wonder 'bout   my   friend,

            D         A         G
    If   he   gave   all   he   could   give.

                        A                    G        D    A
    'Cause he   lived   his   life   like   I   live   mine.

    G                    A              G
      If   you   could   see   inside   my   head,

                    D              A     G
    Then   you   would start   to   under- stand

                    A              G        D    A
    The   things I   value   in   my   heart.
```

Chorus:

```
    G                              D                        A
      And   I   think   it's   al - right      that   I   do   what   I   like

                                        G
    'Cause that's   the   way   I   want   to   live,

    D              A
      It's   how I   give.      And   I'm   still

    G   D   | A   D | G   D   | A   D | G   D | A   D | G   D | A   D ‖
    Giv - ing.
```

Bridge:

```
    C      G        D      A
      You   know that      I   know   that

    C      G      A      D    A
      You're   watching   me.
```

Guitar Solo: *Play 4 times*

```
    ‖: G              A |          | G              D |        A          :‖
```

Chorus:

```
G                           D                           A
    And I   think it's  al - right        that I   do  what I   like

                                          G
    'Cause that's   the   way  I    want  to   live,

D               A
    It's  how I   give.      And I'm   still

G   D   | A   D | G   D | A   D | G   D | A   D | G   D | A   D ‖
Giv - ing.
```

Verse 3:

Bass guitar only.
```
(G)             (D)       (A)       (D)
Gotta make  a   plan, gotta do    what's right.

    (G)             (D)           (A)           (D)
Can't run   around in   circles if   you   wanna build  a    life.

        (G)             (D)           (A)       (D)
But I   don't wanna make  a    plan for  a    day   far  away

        (G)                 (D)           (A)           (D)
While I'm  young and  while I'm  able  all  I    wanna do    is...
```

MARIA

Words by BILLIE JOE
Music by GREEN DAY

Intro:

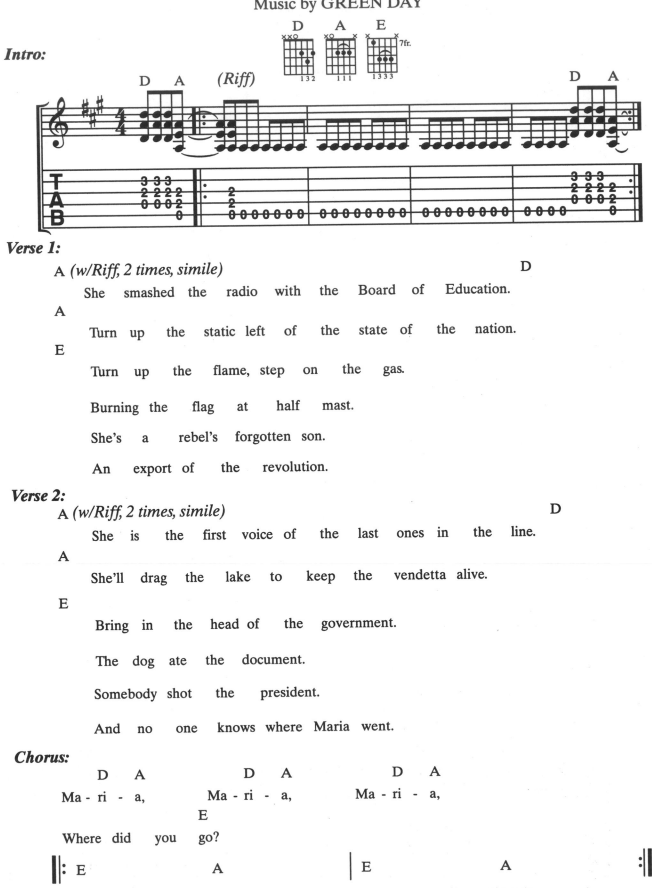

Verse 1:

A *(w/Riff, 2 times, simile)*   D

    She   smashed   the   radio   with   the   Board of   Education.

A

    Turn   up   the   static left   of   the   state of   the   nation.

E

    Turn   up   the   flame, step   on   the   gas.

    Burning   the   flag   at   half   mast.

    She's   a   rebel's   forgotten son.

    An   export   of   the   revolution.

Verse 2:

A *(w/Riff, 2 times, simile)*   D

    She   is   the   first voice   of   the   last   ones   in   the   line.

A

    She'll   drag   the   lake   to   keep   the   vendetta alive.

E

    Bring   in   the   head of   the   government.

    The   dog ate   the   document.

    Somebody shot   the   president.

    And   no   one   knows where Maria went.

Chorus:

    D   A   D   A   D   A

    Ma - ri - a,   Ma - ri - a,   Ma - ri - a,

                  E

    Where   did   you   go?

‖: E   A | E   A   :‖

Bridge:

```
          E      A        E    A
Be   careful  what   you're  offer - ing.
                E          A      E     A
Your   breath  lacks   a    con - viction.
E      A        E         A
Drawing  the  line   in    the   dirt,
          E          A    E
Be - cause  the   last  decision is...
```

Guitar Solo:

‖: D   A | | D   A | | D   A | | E | :‖
   no.

Verse 3:

A *(w/Riff, 2 times, simile)*   D

  She   smashed the radio with the Board of Education.

A

  Turn up   the   static left of   the   state of   the   nation.

E

  Turn up   the   flame, step on   the   gas.

  Burning the   flag   at   half   mast.

  She's   a   rebel's forgotten son.

  An   export of   the   revolution.

Chorus:

```
        D   A         D   A         D   A
Ma - ri - a,     Ma - ri - a,     Ma - ri - a,
                      E
Where did  you   go?
        D   A         D   A         D   A
Ma - ri - a,     Ma - ri - a,     Ma - ri - a,
                      E
Where did  you   go?
```

Outro:

POPROCKS & COKE

Words by BILLIE JOE
Music by GREEN DAY

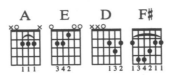

Intro:

4/4 **(Riff)**
A | | | E   ‖

Verse 1:

A   D
Where you go, you know I'll be there.

A   E
If you go far, you know I'll be there.

       D   A
I'll go anywhere, so I'll see you there.

Verse 2:

A   D
You place the name, you know I'll be there.

A   E
You name the time, you know I'll be there.

       D   A
I'll go anywhere, so I'll see you there.

Chorus:

    E   F♯   E
I don't care if you don't mind.

D   A   E   D
I'll be there, not far be - hind.

    A   E   D
I will dare keep in mind.

              A *(w/Riff)*   E
I'll be there for you.

Verse 3:

```
    A                                              D
      When there's a    truth, you   know  I'll   be    there.
    A                                                 E
      Amongst the   lies,  you   know  I'll   be    there.
                   D                 A
    I'll  go   anywhere, so   I'll  see  you  there.
```

Chorus:

```
        E    F#                   E
    I   don't care  if   you   don't mind.
    D    A    E                 D
    I'll  be   there, not   far  be - hind.
        A    E          D
    I   will dare keep in   mind.
                              A (w/Riff)        E
    I'll  be    there for   you.
```

Instrumental:

```
| F#        |      E | A     |        | D     |    | A     |     |      |

| F#        |      E | A     |        | D     |    | E     |     |   ||
```

Verse 4:

```
    A                                              D
      If   you  should fall,  you  know  I'll   be   there.
    A                                                 E
      To   catch the   call,  you  know  I'll   be   there.
                   D                 A
    I'll  go   anywhere, so   I'll  see  you  there.
```

Chorus:

```
        E    F#                    E
    I   don't care  if   you   don't mind.
    D    A    E                 D
    I'll  be   there, not   far  be - hind.
        A    E          D          A    E
    I   will dare keep in   mind.      I   don't care.
                          A          E           A
    I'll  be   there for  you.     I'll  be   there for  you.
        E              A        E   A
    I'll  be   there for  you.
```

SHE

Lyrics by BILLIE JOE
Music by GREEN DAY

Tune down 1/2 step:
⑥ = E♭ ③ = G♭
⑤ = A♭ ② = B♭
④ = D♭ ① = E♭

G   D   C

Intro:

4/4 | Bass Guitar
(G) | | | ‖

Verse 1:

Bass Guitar
(G)   (D)
She,   she   screams   in   silence.

                (C)   (G)
A   sullen   riot   penetrating   through   her   mind.

                         (D)
Waiting   for   a   sign

                                                    Guitar enters
                (C)   G
To   smash   the   silence   with   the   brick   of   self   con - trol.

Chorus:

D   C   G
Are   you   locked   up   in   a   world   that's   been   planned   out   for   you?

D   C   G
Are   you   feeling   like   a   social   tool   without   a   use?

C   G   C   G
Scream   at   me   until   my   ears   bleed.

          C   G   D
I'm   taking   heed   just   for   you.

Verse 2:

G   D
She,   she's   figured   out

          C   G   C   G
All   her   doubts   were   someone   else's   point   of   view.

                    D
Waking   up   this   time

                    C   G   C   G
To   smash   the   silence   with   the   brick   of   self - con - trol.

Chorus:

D   C   G
Are you locked up in a world that's been planned out for you?

D   C   G
Are you feeling like a social tool without a use?

C   G   C   G
Scream at me until my ears bleed.

     C   G   D
I'm taking heed just for you.

Instrumental:

‖: G | | D | | C | | G C G | :‖

Chorus:

D   C   G
Are you locked up in a world that's been planned out for you?

D   C   G
Are you feeling like a social tool without a use?

C   G   C   G
Scream at me until my ears bleed.

     C   G   D   G
I'm taking heed just for you.

GUITAR TAB GLOSSARY **

TABLATURE EXPLANATION

READING TABLATURE: Tablature illustrates the six strings of the guitar. Notes and chords are indicated by the placement of fret numbers on a given string(s).

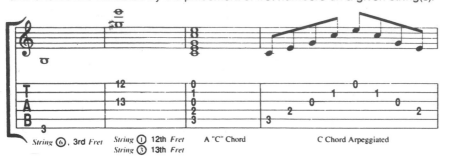

String ⑥, 3rd Fret   String ① 12th Fret   A "C" Chord   C Chord Arpeggiated
String ③ 13th Fret

BENDING NOTES

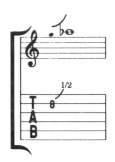

HALF STEP: Play the note and bend string one half step.*

WHOLE STEP: Play the note and bend string one whole step.

PREBEND AND RELEASE: Bend the string, play it, then release to the original note.

RHYTHM SLASHES

STRUM INDICA-TIONS: Strum with indicated rhythm. The chord voicings are found on the first page of the transcription underneath the song title.

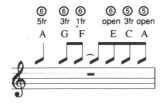

INDICATING SINGLE NOTES USING RHYTHM SLASHES: Very often single notes are incorporated into a rhythm part. The note name is indicated above the rhythm slash with a fret number and a string indication.

*A half step is the smallest interval in Western music; it is equal to one fret. A whole step equals two frets.

**By Kenn Chipkin and Aaron Stang

ARTICULATIONS

HAMMER ON: Play lower note, then "hammer on" to higher note with another finger. Only the first note is attacked.

PULL OFF: Play higher note, then "pull off" to lower note with another finger. Only the first note is attacked.

LEGATO SLIDE: Play note and slide to the following note. (Only first note is attacked).

PALM MUTE: The note or notes are muted by the palm of the pick hand by lightly touching the string(s) near the bridge.

ACCENT: Notes or chords are to be played with added emphasis.

DOWN STROKES AND UPSTROKES: Notes or chords are to be played with either a downstroke (⊓ ·) or upstroke (∨) of the pick.